COUNTRIES OF THE WORLD

CHILE

MARION MORRISON

Evans

TITLES IN THE COUNTRIES OF THE WORLD SERIES:
ARGENTINA • AUSTRALIA • BRAZIL • CANADA • CHILE •
CHINA • EGYPT • FRANCE • GERMANY • INDIA • INDONESIA
ITALY • JAPAN • KENYA • MEXICO • NIGERIA • POLAND
RUSSIA • SOUTH KOREA • SPAIN • SWEDEN • UNITED KINGDOM
USA • VIETNAM

Published by Evans Brothers Limited
2A Portman Mansions
Chiltern Street
London W1U 6NR

VISIT OUR WEBSITE
Evans
www.evansbooks.co.uk

First published 2006
© copyright Evans Brothers 2006

British Library Cataloguing in Publication Data
Morrison, Marion
Chile. – (Countries of the world)
1.Chile – Juvenile literature
I.Title
983'.066

ISBN 0 237 52758 8
13-digit ISBN (from 1 January 2007) 978 0 237 52758 7

Produced for Evans Brothers Limited by
Monkey Puzzle Media Limited
Gissing's Farm, Fressingfield
Suffolk IP21 5SH, UK

Editor: Patience Coster
Designer: Mayer Media Ltd
Map artwork by Peter Bull
Charts and graph artwork by Encompass Graphics Ltd
All photos are by South American Pictures (Danny
Aeberhard, Peter Francis, Robert Francis, David Horwell,
Jason P Howe, Kathy Jarvis, Bill Leimbach, Sue Mann,
Katie Moore, Kimball Morrison, Tony Morrison, Chris
Sharp and Karen Ward) except: Empics 29 (EPA/Ivan
Alvarado).

Endpapers (front): A view over the port and
city of Valparaiso.
Title page: A fruit and vegetable market in
Temuco, the capital of Araucanía region.
Imprint and Contents pages: Estancia Lazo, a
working farm in the Paine district overlooked
by snow-capped Andes Mountains.
Endpapers (back): Salar of San Martin (a salt
lake) and *puna* grasses in the Puna de
Atacama in the northern Andes.

The blue on the Chilean flag represents the clear Andean skies, while the white is for the snow of the mountains. The red band symbolises the blood that was spilled during Chile's fight for independence from Spain, and the star represents the powers of the government.

Snow-capped Andean peaks above rows of vines in the Central Valley.

Chile is one of South America's smaller countries, and certainly its narrowest, shoehorned as it is between the natural boundaries of the Andes Mountains to the east and the Pacific Ocean to the west. In the north, Chile borders with Peru, and to the east with Bolivia and Argentina. A portion of the archipelago of Tierra del Fuego in the south and some Pacific islands are also Chilean territory, and Chile lays claim to part of Antarctica. What Chile lacks in relative size it more than makes up for in the fantastic diversity of its landscape, which encompasses the world's driest desert, immense volcanoes, lush blossom-filled valleys, snowfields, ice caps, grassy savannas and cool temperate rainforests.

The origin of Chile's name is uncertain, but it probably dates from the fifteenth century when Incan armies invaded from the north. The Inca warriors spoke Quechua, a language still spoken by some Andean people today. In Quechua, the word 'chili' refers both to a river and a 'distant place'. Europeans discovered Chile in 1520, when a Portuguese seafarer called Hernando Magellan sighted the southern coast of this beautiful country from his ship. Sixteen years later, Spanish foot soldiers arrived from the north, having overthrown the Inca Empire of Peru. Some of the Spaniards settled in Chile, but the country's natural isolation – guarded by mountains and a formidable desert – meant that only the most determined adventurers managed to invade and remain there. Today's Chileans are descended from Spanish settlers, hardy European immigrants and the largely separate Native American Mapuche people of the south.

A BRUTAL COUP

Chile is often regarded as the most European of all the South American nations and has long been known for political stability and a hardworking European way of life. This image was severely tarnished during the 1970s. In 1973, General Augusto Pinochet seized control of the country in a military coup and installed himself as the leader of a repressive dictatorship. However, Pinochet's government set in motion a major change in the economy. Until the coup, many people had been poor. Although initially they fared little better under Pinochet, from 1988 onwards the number of people living in poverty declined.

KEY DATA

Official Name:	Republic of Chile
Area:	756,950km^2 (including islands but excluding claimed Antarctica)
Population:	15,823,957 (2004 est.)
Main Cities:	Santiago de Chile (capital), Antofagasta, Viña del Mar, Valparaiso, Concepción, Talcahuano
GDP Per Capita:	US$10,274*
Currency:	Chilean peso
Exchange Rate:	US$1 = 580 pesos
	£1 = 1,061 pesos

* (2003) Calculated on Purchasing Power Parity basis
Sources: *CIA World Factbook, 2004;* World Bank

A FERTILE LAND

In the worlds of industry and commerce, Chile possesses plentiful mineral resources, especially copper, for which the country is the world leader. Chile's dynamic agriculture is famed in Western supermarkets, with major exports of fruit and wine to the USA and the European Union and new world markets opening up year upon year. Tourism makes a small though valued contribution to the economy. International visitors enjoy skiing, eco-tourism or take the long flight across the Pacific Ocean to Easter Island to see the curious stone statues carved there centuries ago. Chile relies upon good world prices for its exports, and it has suffered recently because copper prices have been low. At the same time the country's demand for energy has increased, making it a net importer of gas and oil. To add to Chile's woes, the buoyant free market economy has brought more pollution, resulting in an infamous pall of smog that hangs over the city of Santiago for days on end.

Avenida Bernardo O'Higgins, also known as the Alameda, is one of Santiago's busiest streets. Bernardo O'Higgins, of Irish descent, led Chile's fight for independence and became the country's first president.

Cliffs eroded by the sea and the wind line the coast of the northern Atacama Desert.

Chile ranges almost directly north to south through approximately 39 degrees of latitude, or 4,329km. At its widest point, the country is only 380km across and, at its narrowest, a mere 90km. The long, thin mainland of Chile may be divided roughly into three zones. In the north there is the inhospitable Atacama Desert; in the central zone is the capital, Santiago, and a fertile valley that is the nation's agricultural heartland; in the south are deep fjords and glaciers surrounded by cool rainforests. This southern zone includes the desolate archipelago of Tierra del Fuego, which Chile shares with Argentina.

LANDSCAPES OF CHILE
THE GREAT NORTH

The great mountain range of the Andes dominates the land, climate and geological history of Chile. With peaks soaring over 6,000m in height, the Andes are relatively young, unlike many of the world's other great mountain ranges, and are still active as the Earth's crustal plates continue to move. The Nazca plate beneath the floor of the Pacific Ocean is pushing under the South American continental plate, producing volcanic activity and earthquakes. Chile has at least a dozen volcanoes over 6,000m in height, including the world's tallest, Ojos del Salado, which reaches 6,908m.

The mountains rise steeply within a few kilometres of the Chilean coast and the seabed falls away just as abruptly. Close to the city of Antofagasta, the ocean plunges to a depth of 8,064m into a trench that extends along the coast of Chile and Peru. Sea water from the depths of the trench is cooler than

Overlooked by volcanoes, the upper Loa Valley is cultivated with corn, potatoes and other crops.

the oceanic water and it chills the moist air blowing in from the Pacific. This causes thick fog banks to occur over the northern coast for many months of the year. As it reaches the land, the air is unusually cool and is warmed by heat rising from the ground. The warm air absorbs moisture and only in a few places is the fog heavy enough to dampen the earth. This means there is very little rain, so a desert exists that stretches from about 4° South in northern Peru to 26.30° South in Chile. The Chilean section of the desert, the Atacama, is the driest place in the world and rainfall is seldom recorded.

At intervals along Chile's northern coast, 200m-high cliffs rise to plateaus. Here the rocks and coarse sand stretch to the horizon. Further inland, the desert slopes upwards to the volcanoes. Just one river, the Loa, crosses the Atacama, creating a fertile valley. For Chileans this region is *El Norte Grande* – the Great North – a source of copper, the country's main wealth.

Occasionally in the Atacama Desert it rains locally and heavily for just a few hours. Within days, thousands of seeds that have lain dormant from a previous flowering period germinate. The plants grow quickly, then flower and die.

CASE STUDY
CATCHING FOG

Water is very precious to people living in the Atacama region. While engineers have laid a pipeline measuring more than 200km from the Andes Mountains to supply the city and port of Antofagasta, small settlements often have to rely on supplies carried by road tankers. So an ingenious idea of catching the *camanchaca*, or fog, has been developed. At the small settlement of Falda Verde, the annual precipitation from rain and dew is only 30mm. The people living there have erected fine, plastic nets on poles on a cliff 600m above the village to catch the fog, which condenses on the mesh in the same way that dew collects on a spider's web. Fog droplets gather and run down the net into plastic collectors and are then piped to a greenhouse and used for growing tomatoes.

LANDSCAPE FEATURES

PERU

BOLIVIA

ATACAMA DESERT

LOA RIVER

Llullaillaco volcano (6,723m)

Mt. Ojos del Salado (6,908m)

ANDES

N

Río Bío

Villarica volcano (2,840m)

Lake District

Osorno volcano (2,660m)

Lago Todos los Santos

Chiloé Island

0   500km
0   300 miles

Continental Ice Cap (North)

Continental Ice Cap (South)

Strait of Magellan

Tierra del Fuego

Mt. Darwin (2,438m)

Cape Horn

LITTLE NORTH

About 900km south of the border with Peru, the Atacama Desert mellows, giving way to some vegetation. Chileans know this region as *Norte Chico*, or Little North. It extends southwards for roughly 600km, from the town of Chañaral to Illapel, approximately 200km north of Santiago. The changes in the vegetation are gradual and traces of the desert are everywhere. In this region, several rivers flow the short distance from the Andes to the Pacific. These rivers, some of which are just seasonal, pass through fertile valleys. The old colonial town of La Serena, famed for its beauty and climate, lies in the Elqui Valley.

CENTRAL VALLEY

Southwards from Illapel the landscape changes as the Cordillera de la Costa, an outlying low range of the Andes, gives rise to numerous valleys in which people have settled. The Cordillera de la Costa causes moist air coming from the sea to rise, cool and then fall as rain, resulting in agriculturally productive land.

Ninety per cent of Chile's people live in the central region. Most reside in Santiago, which is situated in the Central Valley at an altitude of 520m between the Andes and the Cordillera de la Costa. The Central Valley is a long, narrow plain hemmed in by the Andes and crossed by several rivers. It runs south from Santiago for around 450km and its southern frontier is the 380km-long Bío Bío River, which drains north-westward into the Pacific at the major port of Concepción. Intensive farming has completely changed the original forest

REGIONS OF CHILE

A fine colonial building, the Tribunales de Justicia, graces the town of La Serena. The cathedral is visible in the far right of the photo.

vegetation of the valley. Orchards, vineyards and pastures lie within this region, as do two of Chile's larger cities, Rancagua and Talca.

The fertile Central Valley is intensively cultivated. Here an almond orchard grows in the shadow of the mountains.

CASE STUDY
THE 1960 EARTHQUAKE

At about 6 am on Saturday 21 May 1960, the first tremors of a huge earthquake were felt in the central and southern regions. Aftershocks followed and continued until Sunday afternoon, when another shock larger than the first struck, causing extensive damage. People rushed into the streets in fear of their lives and were still outside when the third major shock occurred. This was twenty times more powerful than the first, lasting three minutes and causing major damage and changes to the landscape. Before the earthquake, Valdivia had been a river port. Afterwards it became a seaport – this was because 390km^2 of land had subsided. But the worst was not over; onlookers saw the ocean retreat to leave boats standing high and dry on the shore. Then, about fifteen minutes later, the first of a series of tsunamis, or great sea surges, arrived and rushed nearly 3km inland. The wall of water was 6m high and the first wave was followed by more, the fourth being the highest. This immense earthquake had a magnitude of 9.5 on the Richter scale. Many experts consider it to have been the world's greatest in recorded history, not so much for loss of life but for the effect it had on the landscape. The shock was so violent that it set the Earth 'ringing' with vibrations detected for two weeks after the event and recorded by seismometers around the world. Estimates suggest that more than 2,000 people died, 3,000 were injured and two million lost their homes in the earthquake.

THE SOUTH

The region that extends from the Bío Bío River some 350km south to Puerto Montt is known as Chile's Lake District and contains some of the country's finest farmland. This is a spectacular landscape of beautiful, mostly glacial lakes, some of which, like Lago Todos Los Santos, are a deep emerald-green colour. Rainfall is high and waterfalls abound. Snowcapped volcanoes, including the perfectly conical Osorno (2,660m), surround the lakes. Some of these volcanoes, like Volcán Villarica (2,840m), are active, with craters of red-hot lava emitting large clouds of smoke. The Lake District was once an area of dense forest, and Chilean pines still flourish here, as do the last of the *alerce* trees, evergreen conifers which are some 3,000 to 4,000 years old. The government has created several national parks, including the Parque Nacional Alerce Andino, to preserve the area's rare wildlife and flora.

PATAGONIA

To the south, the Lake District gives way to a coastline of narrow fjords and inlets some hundreds of kilometres long. The deep fjords lead far into the mountains and are the result

ABOVE: Volcán Osorno, one of the many impressive volcanoes in the Lake District, towers over the Petrohue Falls in the foreground.

BELOW: Chile has many active volcanoes. Smoke and steam pour from a new eruptive cone on the side of Volcán Lonquimay.

The Chiloé archipelago, which consists of one major island, Isla Grande, and more than a dozen smaller ones, was isolated from the rest of Chile for many years. The people who settled there lived on local resources by fishing and farming. The islanders were the last supporters of the Spanish Crown in South America. In the 1800s, the last Spanish governor fled to Isla Grande to escape a rebellion on the mainland. The islanders' self-sufficient way of life gradually became the stuff of legend and Chiloé developed a reputation as a kind of mystical paradise. The story has survived to this day, and each year an ever-increasing number of tourists are inspired to visit the pure waters, dense forests (some of which are now reserves) and the 150 or so churches left behind by Jesuits and other missionaries.

Shoppers and traders at the market in Castro on Isla Grande, Chiloé.

of glaciation that began during the Pleistocene period some 1.5 million years ago. The dramatic coastline is enormously fragmented with hundreds of small islands, many of which are uninhabited.

Much of the lowland is cool temperate rainforest, one of the largest areas of its kind left in the world. At a higher level, the land is covered by two vast ice caps, the Northern and Southern ice fields of the Patagonian Ice Cap, which effectively cut off southern Chile from the rest of the country. In parts of the Northern Ice Field the ice is more than 1,400m thick. At this latitude, the Andes are lower and glaciers move down to the sea. In the far south, thousands of tourists trek every year to see mountains that have been eroded into fantastic shapes by the ice.

Chile's mainland terminates on the northern shore of the Strait of Magellan, named after the Portuguese navigator. The strait is controlled by Chile and is the principal southern route between the Atlantic and Pacific oceans. The Chilean border extends eastward to the Atlantic coast, where Chile has approximately 3km of shoreline.

THE DISAPPEARING GLACIER OF SAN RAFAEL

For some time, scientists have warned of the dangerous effects of rising temperatures on one of Chile's greatest tourist attractions. Global warming is melting the awesome San Rafael glacier. At sea level, the glacier's 70m-high front wall meets the Laguna San Rafael. Vast blocks of ice shear off and fall into the lagoon with a colossal splash. This region of spectacular forests in an icy landscape has been declared a World Heritage site and UNESCO biosphere reserve. The glacier used to be much larger, but its front wall now stands 1km further back than it did in the early 1990s.

This so-called 'banner tree' has been shaped by the strong winds on Tierra del Fuego.

TIERRA DEL FUEGO

Chile owns about two thirds of the archipelago of Tierra del Fuego, or Land of Fire, which lies across the Magellan Strait in the far south. The eastern part of the archipelago is made up of one large island, the Isla Grande, while the western part is fragmented with numerous small islands and channels. The name Tierra del Fuego derives from explorers' reports of the fires that were made by Native Americans living along the shore. The eastern part, which is largely flat and used for sheep farming, belongs to Argentina. The western, Chilean part is wild and dominated by the southernmost ridges of the Andean mountain chain. The Cordillera Darwin, a range of mountains named after the Victorian naturalist explorer, Charles Darwin, extends along the southern edge and Mount Darwin (2,438m) is the highest point. The most southerly point is Cape Horn Island (apart from the two small islands of Diego Ramiréz, which lie a further 100km to the south-west). Chile also claims a sector of Antarctica covering an area of 1,250,000km².

PACIFIC ISLANDS

Easter Island, or *Isla de Pascua*, is situated in the Pacific about 3,600km west of Chile and has a history of volcanic activity. The population is made up of people of Polynesian descent, who call the island 'Rapa Nui'. Easter Island is often regarded as the world's most remote island and is famous for the centuries-old gigantic heads carved in stone.

The Juan Fernández group consists of three islands lying about 600km west of Valparaíso. Other islands include the small and uninhabited Sala y Goméz, which is 400km east of Easter Island, and San Ambrosio and San Félix, which lie 1,000km north-west of Valparaíso and 20km apart.

CLIMATE

Chile has one of the most extraordinary climates in the world. The vast range of latitude and altitude of the mainland, the unusual influences of the cooling Pacific Ocean in the north and high rainfall in the south all contribute to the huge variations from region to region. The Atacama area is parched and, in places, the surface closely resembles that of Mars. The lower regions of the country are dry and often warm while the higher regions are baking hot in the day and bitterly cold at night. The Central Valley is more temperate, but the higher mountains are cooler and mostly snow-covered. And the wild sea and violent winds around Cape Horn have long had a treacherous and deadly reputation among sailors.

Giant stone carved statues, or *moai*, stand on a stone platform on Easter Island.

TEMPERATURE AND RAINFALL

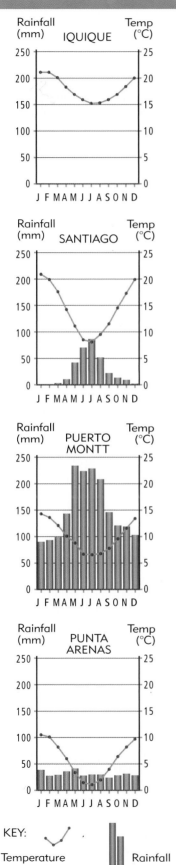

Rainfall (mm) / Temp (°C) — IQUIQUE

Rainfall (mm) / Temp (°C) — SANTIAGO

Rainfall (mm) / Temp (°C) — PUERTO MONTT

Rainfall (mm) / Temp (°C) — PUNTA ARENAS

KEY:
Temperature   Rainfall

El Niño is an upwelling of warm water in the tropical Pacific that disrupts the ocean-atmosphere system. This warming of oceanic water (in Chile normally between December and February) can have devastating consequences. It brings a change in climate to many parts of the world and, in particular, rain to the deserts of western South America. El Niño (meaning 'boy child') was given its name in Spanish colonial times by fishermen who noticed unusual warming of the sea during December. They called it El Niño after the birth of Jesus Christ. In 1997, El Niño accounted for at least 2,100 deaths and billions of dollars worth of property damage around the world. Although some of the strongest effects resulted in heavy floods in Peru and Ecuador, Chile suffered freak storms and flooding. Santiago received ten times the average rainfall and five major storms swept the Central Valley. In the north, the fishing harvest was reduced, pelicans invaded the city of Arica, and snow in the mountains was heavier than usual.

As a result of El Niño, brown pelicans flock to the coast in search of food.

17

Most Chileans have European and Native American ancestry.

Chile has a population of almost 16 million people, about 90 per cent of whom live in the central region. Over 86 per cent of Chileans live in cities; a third of the total population lives in the capital, Santiago. Most Chileans are of European or European and Native American descent. The rest of the population is made up of Europeans and other immigrants, together with a few Native Americans.

FIRST PEOPLES

Humans arrived in the far south of the Americas around 12,000 BC. By 500 BC, various groups had settled and were cultivating basic crops including maize and potatoes. Around AD 300, groups in the central region included the Molle and the Llolleo, who cultivated maize, beans and squash and supplemented their diet by fishing and hunting. In AD 1000, the Aconcagua and the Diaguita dominated the region, the latter group producing fine pottery with white, red and black designs.

Most remarkable of the tribes in the south were the Mapuche. They were part of a much larger group, known as the Araucanians, who at one time also occupied the Central Valley region. In the far south, peoples such as the Yámana, Selk'nam and Tehuelche led a primitive existence, fishing among the icy fjords and hunting on the windswept Patagonian plains. The great Inca civilisation of Peru expanded into northern Chile in the late fifteenth century. The Incas conquered the north part of the country, but were unable to defeat the Mapuche, who put up fierce resistance and prevented them from expanding their empire south of the River Maule.

A Mapuche family photographed in the late nineteenth century. The Mapuche are the largest indigenous group in Chile today.

POPULATION, 1950–2050

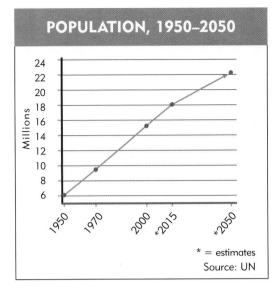

* = estimates
Source: UN

THE SPANISH CONQUEST

In 1532, Spanish conquistadors arrived in Peru, and with their superior weaponry and horses defeated the Incas. The conquistadors made expeditions into Chile. In 1541, Pedro de Valdivia founded Santiago de la Nueva Extremadura as the capital of the new colony. Like the Incas, however, the Spanish soldiers were unable to conquer the Mapuche, and their influence extended no further south than the Bío Bío River.

The Spaniards ruled Chile north of the Bío Bío River for almost three hundred years. But their interest in this isolated colony was limited as they did not find gold or silver there. Most of the few Spanish settlers became farmers, and thus brought about the indigenous population's decline. Some Native Americans were forced to work as slaves, but the majority died in warfare or from diseases that the settlers had unwittingly brought from Europe. The Mapuche survived and, although their territory was reduced, they never became part of the Spanish colony. In 1818, Chile declared its independence from Spain. From about 1845, immigrants were encouraged to settle, and many arrived from Europe and the Middle East during the nineteenth and twentieth centuries.

In 1983, workers laying pipes in the Atacama found a burial site of Chinchorro mummies. Some of these were 7,000 years old and therefore the oldest mummies in the world. The Chinchorros lived around 7,800 to 3,800 years ago and were simple hunter-gatherers, but they understood sophisticated mummification techniques. These skills involved removing the brain and internal organs from a dead body, strengthening the bones with sticks and binding them into place with reeds. The body cavity was dried out with hot stones or fire and re-filled with straw and ashes before being stitched up. The face was covered with a hard paste in which the eyes, nose and mouth were marked, and the mummy was given a wig of human hair. The Chinchorros performed this custom until about 1,500 BC when, for unknown reasons, it came to an end.

Ninety-six bodies were found in the Chinchorro burial site. A woman is one of the four now preserved in a museum near Arica.

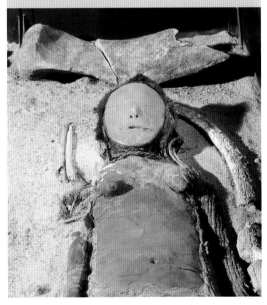

CHILEANS TODAY

Most of the Spanish settlers to Chile were men without families. With the indigenous women, these men produced a people of mixed race, the *mestizos*, the descendants of whom constitute the majority of Chileans today. Most Chileans have dark hair and brown eyes, and skin colour ranges from light to dark. Compared with countries like Argentina, Chile only received a small number of immigrants, and they have not greatly affected the physical appearance of Chileans. The indigenous population is small, less than 3 per cent, and is largely identified by clothing, language and last names, which are clearly not Spanish.

INDIGENOUS PEOPLES

With a population of about 400,000, Mapuche groups make up 90 per cent of Chile's indigenous people. They include the Pehuenche and the Huilliche. In 1883, the Chile authorities finally and brutally defeated the Mapuche, who lost their land and were for the most part placed in reservations. Mapuche means 'people of the land', but today about a third of them live in urban areas. They have their own language, 'Mapudungu', but more than 90 per cent speak Spanish. Some of them have received a modest schooling and can read and write. Those on reservations are very poor and live by farming, hunting and gathering. The Pehuenche harvest *araucaria* pine nuts and trade them for other goods.

During the 1980s, the repressive military regime did not allow the Mapuche to practise their religion or customs, or speak their language in public. The Mapuche protested

Mapuches often travel by horse and cart as the roads in their communities are unpaved.

and formed organisations to demand the return of their land, but their public meetings were disrupted and some members were murdered. Recent governments have been more tolerant and have met some of the Mapuche demands.

Chile's second largest indigenous group is the Aymara, together with a few Quechua who live in the far north. Estimates vary as to their number, which could be around 40,000. They are related to the much larger groups of Aymara and Quechua of Bolivia and Peru. Traditionally they live in the Andes Mountains, in houses of mud and straw, and grow potatoes and cereals and raise llamas and alpacas. In recent decades, many have left the highlands and moved to towns on the coast. They wear Western clothing, pursue a Western lifestyle and essentially can be classed as *mestizos*. Most of them speak Spanish but they also preserve their own Aymara and Quechua languages, and many of them keep houses in the mountains and return there for festivals and to see their families.

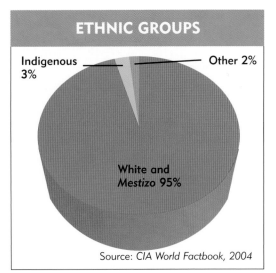

ETHNIC GROUPS

Indigenous 3%

Other 2%

White and Mestizo 95%

Source: CIA World Factbook, 2004

The tribes of the far south of Chile have almost died out, though there may be one or two Yámana speakers left. They survived to the end of the nineteenth century, their simple lifestyle virtually unchanged until the arrival of seal hunters, gold prospectors and sheep farmers who opened up the area, settled on their land, and brought diseases to which the tribes had no immunity.

CASE STUDY
POLYNESIANS OF EASTER ISLAND

Some 3,500 people live on Easter Island, of whom about 70 per cent are native *Pascuenses* (*Pascua* is Spanish for 'Easter'). The remainder are immigrants from mainland Chile. Most *Pascuenses* are of Polynesian descent and speak their own Polynesian-based language as well as Spanish. In the nineteenth century, the population almost became extinct when the majority of *Pascuenses* were forced to leave the island to work in mines in Peru. Others died from disease. In 1888, Easter Island officially became Chilean, but it was not until 1964 that the people were recognised as Chilean citizens and given the right to vote. Today most of the *Pascuenses* live in the single settlement of Hanga Roa, and make their living from tourism.

A young man of Polynesian descent from Easter Island. Most experts believe the Polynesians arrived some time before AD 800.

IMMIGRANTS

Some of the first immigrants were Germans, who arrived in the mid-nineteenth century and settled in the Lake District. They gradually transformed the area between Valdivia and Puerto Montt into some of the finest dairy farmland in Chile. They brought industry to Valdivia, founding shipyards, breweries and mills. Despite suffering many earthquakes, Valdivia still has some German churches and buildings. Around Lago Llanquihue some third-generation immigrants speak German at home. Other immigrants included Scots and English people, who were involved in business and sheep farming. Chilean governments of the day preferred the culture and knowledge of white European immigrants, and although the immigrant community was small it had a considerable impact on the country's economic and cultural development.

Towards the end of the nineteenth century, immigrants arrived from Italy, France, Switzerland and Croatia. They were followed early in the twentieth century by Jews from Germany and Eastern Europe, and Christians from Lebanon, Palestine and Syria, all of whom were fleeing persecution or conflicts in their own countries. None of the groups was

European-style buildings on the riverfront at Valdivia, where many German immigrants settled.

large, and together they never made up more than 10 per cent of the population. They integrated well, and by the second generation considered themselves as Chileans. Today the Jewish community numbers about 21,000 and the majority live in Santiago, where there is a large Jewish school. There is also a tiny population of about 3,000 Muslims.

Recently, the largest influx of immigrants has come from the neighbouring countries of Argentina, Peru and Bolivia and other Latin American countries. Many of these are illegal entrants, attracted by better political and economic conditions in Chile. Workers from Peru, in particular, are prepared to take on low-paid, menial jobs and there is concern that they are being exploited.

EMIGRANTS

In the 1950s, an oil boom in Argentina's Patagonia attracted large numbers of Chilean workers. Most came from towns in Chile's south, and the island of Chiloé. Argentina has the largest Chilean population overseas, at over 160,000. In the early days, most Chileans

URBAN POPULATION

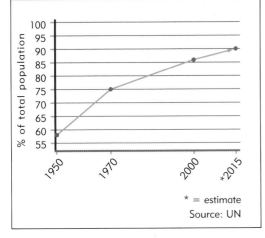

* = estimate
Source: UN

In 1865, some 115,4000 people (just over 6 per cent of Chile's population) lived in Santiago. Early in the twentieth century, industrialisation attracted workers and by 1950 the population had soared to 1.33 million. Twenty years later the population had more than doubled to 2.84 million, and by 2002 it had almost doubled again to 4.6 million. Metropolitan or Greater Santiago is now home to over one third of Chile's population. Much of this rapid growth is the result of people moving from rural areas in search of a better life. This has put a great strain on the city's housing, schools, hospitals and employment. New arrivals have been forced to live in crowded conditions with relatives or in makeshift shanties on the outskirts of the city. The authorities have tried to solve the problem with alternative low-income housing and most areas now have access to electricity, running water and sanitation. Primary schools have kept pace with the increased numbers, but poorer people still have problems accessing medical care and finding employment.

in Argentina were labourers, but now those who emigrate are highly qualified. During the repressive regime of General Pinochet, between 1973 and 1990, more than 500,000 Chileans voluntarily left or were forced to flee the country. Many went to Europe, Australia, Canada and Venezuela, as well as Argentina. Some emigrants have returned, but it is estimated that around 800,000 Chileans live abroad.

It is estimated that Santiago's population of about 5 million people will grow to over 6 million by the year 2015.

POPULATION

During the twentieth century, Chile's population grew steadily at an annual rate of about 1 per cent. In 1900, the population was about three million, by 1950 it had reached just over six million and, in 2000, was approximately 15.2 million. The growth rate is expected to remain much the same, a little over 1 per cent, and on that basis the population is likely to exceed 20 million by 2030. Most of the growth has been in urban areas, while rural areas remain reasonably static. For example, in 1985 the urban population was almost ten million, and the rural population about two million. In 2025, it is expected that the urban population will be 17.3 million with the rural still around 2.2 million. The small rise in the rural population is partly because of increased employment opportunities in the fishing and mining industries in the north and south of the country.

POPULATION DISTRIBUTION

About 90 per cent of Chileans live in the central region of Chile between La Serena and Puerto Montt. The Central Valley is the most densely populated area. With the exception of metropolitan Santiago and Valparaiso, however, nowhere does population exceed 55 persons per square kilometre. The average for the country is 19.9 per square kilometre, but vast areas north and south of the central region are virtually uninhabited. The average for most of the Atacama region north of La Serena, and for much of the region south of Puerto Montt, is fewer than five persons per square kilometre.

There has been a worldwide trend, especially in developing countries, for people to move from rural areas into towns and cities in search of work and better educational and medical facilities. Since the 1930s, the majority of Chileans have lived in towns and cities. Eighty-six per cent of Chileans now live in urban centres (towns with a population greater than 20,000 inhabitants). Only two of the top ten largest urban centres – Antofagasta and Iquique – are located outside the central region, in the north. Metropolitan Santiago has become so large that two of its suburbs, Puente Alto and San Bernardino, are considered to be two of the country's largest cities.

Children pose for the camera in a playground in a coastal Atacama village in north Chile. The Atacama region is relatively sparsely populated.

POPULATION DENSITY

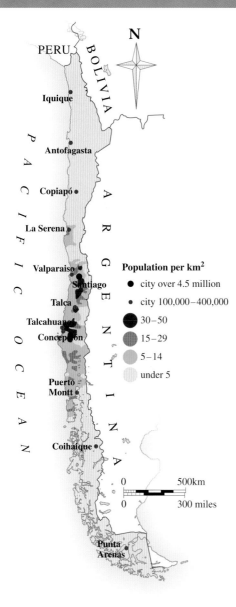

Population per km²

- ● city over 4.5 million
- • city 100,000–400,000
- ● 30–50
- ● 15–29
- ● 5–14
- under 5

0   500km
0   300 miles

People leave rural areas to seek work in the cities. Here a man sits by the roadside in La Serena making wickerwork dolls, crosses and baskets.

POPULATION STRUCTURE, 2004

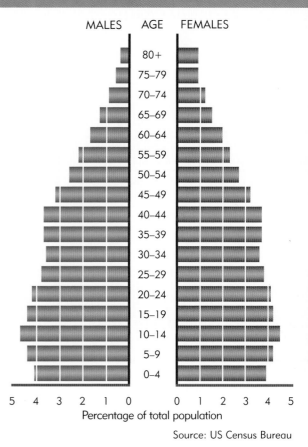

Source: US Census Bureau

POPULATION STRUCTURE

Chile's steady growth over the last one hundred years has led to a society that is almost evenly divided between men and women. The majority of the population – almost two thirds – are between the ages of 14 and 65. This is likely to change in the future, but only gradually. In recent decades, and largely as a result of better medical care and dietary habits, people are living longer. Between 1965 and 1970, men could expect an average life of about 59 years, and women of 63 years. Within the last forty years this average has increased to about 72 years for men and 80 years for women. This reflects a worldwide trend that will produce a greater percentage of the elderly in the population.

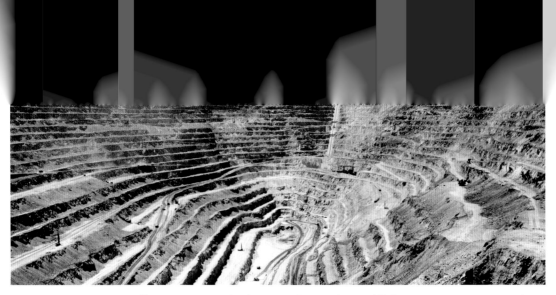

Chuquicamata in the Atacama Desert, the world's largest open-pit copper mine.

Industry employs 23.4 per cent of the labour force and contributes 38.8 per cent to GNP (gross national product). Chile is the world's leading copper exporter, with some of the largest reserves in existence; it also has massive mineral reserves.

A few years ago, copper production pulled the country back from the brink of recession, and the 'economic miracle' started in the Pinochet years has benefited industry as a whole. Pinochet introduced a free market economy, reduced the role of government in industry, and encouraged investment from foreign companies. Between 1973 and 1981 inflation fell from 900 per cent to 9.5 per cent; but to achieve this the government borrowed from international banks and governments and, by the early 1980s, the country was heavily in debt. The debt crisis was resolved in the late 1980s and Pinochet's economic measures once again brought the country prosperity.

RED GOLD OF THE ANDES

Mineral prospectors have been attracted to the Andes since the Spanish invasion of the sixteenth century. In the early 1900s, major North American companies controlled many of the great copper mines. In 1965, however, the government of Eduardo Frei set in motion a plan to nationalise the five largest mines, which are now controlled by CODELCO, the National Copper Corporation, and form the backbone of the Chilean economy. In the

Andes to the east of the Central Valley, El Teniente is the world's largest underground copper mine with 2,400km of tunnels. Chuquicamata, set in the Atacama Desert at an altitude of 2,830m–3,000m, is the world's largest open-pit copper mine.

MINERALS AND SEMI-PRECIOUS STONES

Other minerals found in Chile include large deposits of iron ore, nitrates, iodine, sulphur and manganese. After Bolivia, Chile has the world's largest reserve of lithium (40 per cent), and is estimated to have one fifth of the world's molybdenum, a metal used in the manufacture of high-tensile steel and specialised lubricants.

Semi-precious stones found in Chile include the deep blue lapis lazuli, used for making jewellery. Afghanistan is the only other serious source of lapis. Onyx, agate, amethyst and the precious metals gold and silver are also mined. Chile boasts the world's highest mine, located near the summit of the volcano Aucanquilcha (6,176m), where natural sulphur was dug until recently. A handful of hardy miners working without oxygen also dug for *covelite*, a green copper mineral used to make jewellery.

CASE STUDY
THE NITRATE AGE OF BOOM AND BUST

The second half of the nineteenth century was an era of prosperity for the northern coast of Chile. Millions of pounds were invested largely by the UK to extract a mineral known as *caliche* in the desert. This dull brown rock is rich in nitrates, particularly saltpetre (sodium nitrate) and was in demand for making explosives and as an agricultural fertiliser. The extraordinary climate of the Chilean desert prevents the nitrates from leaching away, so they remain in beds varying from a simple crust to a metre or more in thickness. Towns, extraction plants and railways were established to support the nitrate industry. From 1879 to 1883, the War of the Pacific was fought between Chile, Bolivia and Peru over nitrate-rich territory in the northern Atacama Desert. By the start of the twentieth century, however, scientists had developed other ways of making artificial fertiliser and explosives. The Chilean nitrate economy finally collapsed in the world depression of the 1930s, leaving ghost towns around the derelict plants.

Humberstone, an abandoned nitrate plant.

MINERALS AND ENERGY

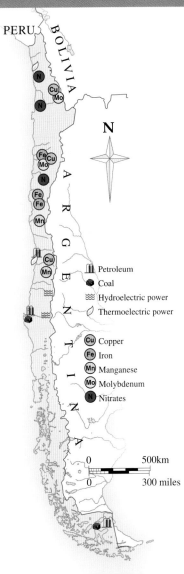

Petroleum
Coal
Hydroelectric power
Thermoelectric power

Cu Copper
Fe Iron
Mn Manganese
Mo Molybdenum
N Nitrates

0   500km
0   300 miles

An oil drilling rig in the Magellan Strait, close to the city of Punta Arenas.

Chile's largest coal mine near Valdivia closed in 1997 and Chile has become a net importer, with supplies crossing the Pacific from Australia. Chile has vast hydroelectric (HEP) potential because of its many rivers, and HEP has long been the principal source of electrical energy. But HEP is affected by droughts and in 1997 a severe drought caused frequent power cuts in Santiago. The government has sought alternative sources of power while continuing to build HEP stations in the wetter areas. One scheme in Bío Bío has come under attack from environmentalists and indigenous people.

ENERGY

While Chile has an abundance of natural resources, it is short of energy, supplying only 40 per cent of its national energy requirements. In 2001, 17 per cent of the value of Chile's imports was made up of fuel and energy. Although oil, gas and coal occur naturally, they are insufficient for the needs of an expanding economy. The reserves are in Tierra del Fuego, in a geological structure known as the Magallanes Basin. Chile produces little oil, and in recent years production has declined, leaving no alternative other than to import. Between 1982 and 2002, the number of barrels produced a day fell from 54,000 to 14,000, while consumption increased by about 135 per cent. Chile has three refineries, the largest near the city and port of Talcahuano. Oil is carried from the refineries across the country through a network of pipelines. Between 1997 and 2001, natural gas production also declined by 44 per cent. Chile needs gas for use in power stations to generate electricity for urban areas, and for fuelling copper smelters. The government has promoted the use of natural gas and, since 1997, has imported large amounts from Argentina. As a result, gas consumption has grown rapidly.

The coal reserves in Tierra del Fuego are large in proportion to demand, but in recent years production has declined because of rising costs.

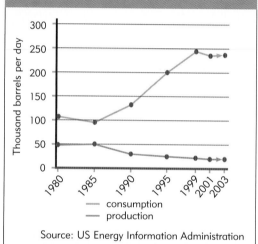

OIL PRODUCTION AND CONSUMPTION, 1980–2003

Source: US Energy Information Administration

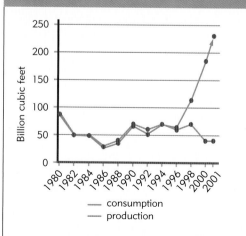

NATURAL GAS PRODUCTION AND CONSUMPTION, 1980–2001

Source: US Energy Information Administration

GNI PER CAPITA (US$)

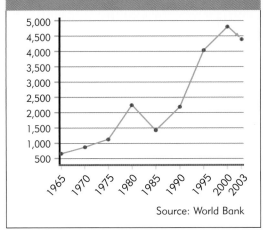

Source: World Bank

ELECTRICITY GENERATION, 1980–2002

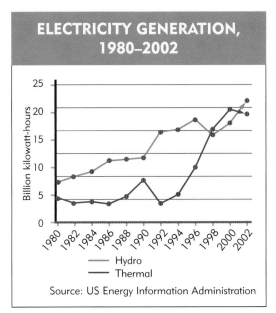

— Hydro
— Thermal

Source: US Energy Information Administration

GEOTHERMAL ENERGY

In Chile, as in many countries around the world, clean, environment-friendly projects receive priority attention. One such project involves accessing energy sources trapped in the ground in volcanic regions. The Atacama, in particular, is noted for hot springs and geysers where steam billows from holes in the ground, and sometimes water gushes out too. Pipes are set in the warm rock to tap the water and steam, which are then used either directly to heat homes or generate electrical power for distribution. One drawback is the cost, particularly when some sources are unpredictable: geyser pressures and temperatures do not always last.

The Bío Bío River rises in the Andes in a region of small lakes and forests and flows 380km to the Pacific. Along its course, one million people depend upon the river for agriculture, fishing and tourism. In the late 1980s, a plan to dam the river for HEP was immediately opposed by environmentalists, not least because the project would displace 600 Pehuenche people. During the late 1990s, the project was delayed by court actions and by four elderly Pehuenche women who refused to leave their homes. Eventually the controversial scheme moved ahead and Ralco, the largest of several dams, was completed. In April 2004, ENDESA, the Chilean energy company responsible for the work announced that the reservoir would be filled by August 2004. ENDESA predicted that soon afterwards the production of 547 megawatts of power would begin. Despite continuing opposition, the reservoir has now been created.

BELOW: A Pehuenche man walks past the reservoir of the Ralco Dam, shortly after its completion in 2004.

MANUFACTURING

Chile is developing a small and efficient manufacturing industry that provides for its own people, together with markets in neighbouring South American countries. It is based on local mineral resources, agricultural raw materials and forestry. Industries include copper and oil refining, nitrate products, and the manufacture of cement and various building materials. There are large iron smelting and steel production plants in Santiago and Concepción.

Other products include packaging in plastic and other materials, pharmaceutical and health products, and household items such as refrigerators and ovens. There is a thriving leather industry, and manufacture of textiles and clothing is wide-ranging. Perhaps the most important manufactured goods are food products, which include meat, sugar, wine and beer. There is a small, growing automobile and light van production industry. While Concepción and Valdivia are major industrial centres, 75 per cent of manufacturing is centred on Santiago and Valparaiso. The government is encouraging the establishment of new industries in sparsely inhabited regions, especially in the south.

SERVICE INDUSTRY

Services industries employ about 63 per cent of the labour force and contribute 55 per cent to GDP. Service industries include financial institutions such as banks, stock exchanges and insurance companies. These are mostly based in Santiago but have subsidiaries in major towns in the north and south. Tourism has also created many service industry jobs. People are employed in numerous hotels, restaurants and roadside facilities, as guides for trekking and in campsites, tour agencies, riding stables, white-water rafting and boating marinas. The service industry also includes transport, telecommunications, computer-processing and government-run programmes such as public health and education.

EXPORTS AND IMPORTS

Chile's economy has the best rating of all Latin American countries. It is highly dependent on international trade. Chile has signed free trade agreements with many countries, including the USA (effective as of January 2004), Canada and the European Union. It is also a member of the Asian-Pacific Economic Cooperation Group Community, and an associate member of MERCOSUR, the Southern Common Market, formed by Argentina, Brazil, Paraguay and Uruguay. According to the anti-corruption organisation Transparency International, Chile

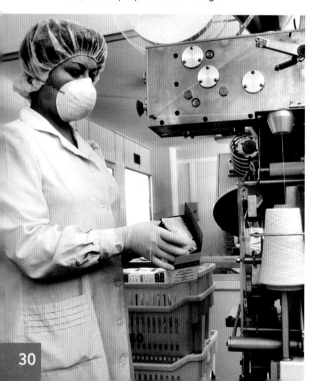

A young woman at work in the pharmaceutical industry, where modern equipment ensures safe, clean preparation of drugs.

is the least corrupt country in Latin America. This is an important factor for foreigners and others wishing to invest in the economy.

Chile's main exports are copper, fish, fruits, paper and pulp, chemicals and wine. Imports include consumer goods, chemicals, motor vehicles, fuels, and electrical and heavy industrial machinery. For 2003, total estimated exports were $20.44 billion, and imports were $17.4 billion. The USA is the main export market and buys about one fifth of all Chile's exports, although in recent years China's need for copper has exceeded that of the USA. Asia is becoming an increasingly important market, accounting for about a third of Chile's total exports. In the first seven months of 2004, exports to Asia increased by over 60 per cent compared with 2003. In particular, exports to South Korea rose by over 80 per cent following the signing of a free trade agreement.

In 2001, mining contributed 40.1 per cent of total export earnings. Of this, copper represented 25.7 per cent, a reduction from previous years. The contribution to exports from the agricultural and services industries has increased to around 60 per cent. Most of Chile's foreign trade is carried by ship, and the five major ports are Valparaiso, Talcahuano, Antofagasta, San Antonio and Arica.

RIGHT: Valparaiso, one of Chile's main ports, handles thousands of shipping containers a year.

VALUE OF EXPORTS AND IMPORTS (BILLION US$)

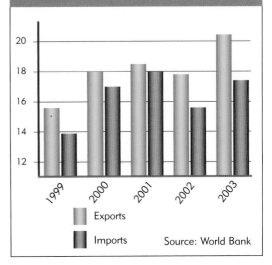

Exports

Imports   Source: World Bank

MAJOR TRADING PARTNERS (% OF VALUE), 2003

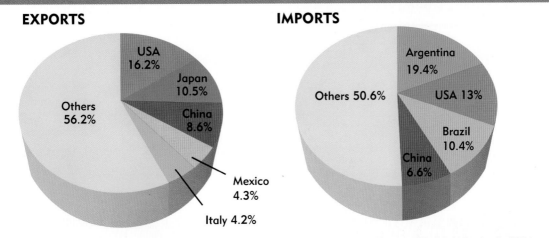

EXPORTS

USA 16.2%
Japan 10.5%
China 8.6%
Others 56.2%
Mexico 4.3%
Italy 4.2%

IMPORTS

Argentina 19.4%
USA 13%
Others 50.6%
Brazil 10.4%
China 6.6%

Source: *CIA World Factbook, 2004*

31

TOURISM

Chile is attracting increasing numbers of tourists. During the summer months in particular, most holidaymakers head for the Lake District and Patagonia. These regions are ideally suited to adventure tourism, with white-water rafting, kayaking in the fjords, trekking through lush forests and volcano climbing. A popular destination is the Towers of Paine National Park with spectacularly eroded mountains and glacial lakes that can only be reached by roads starting in the south or from neighbouring Argentina. The park is always busy with campers and specialised tour groups as the mountains are only accessible by boat and clearly marked trails.

Skiing has always attracted enthusiasts from around the world and many from neighbouring Argentina. Portillo, about 120km from Santiago, is the most famous resort. The northern area also attracts many foreign visitors. The desolate regions of the Atacama boast volcanoes, fine beaches, strange plants and rare animals and appeal to travellers from the crowded towns of Europe and the USA.

In 2000, income from tourism totalled US$827 million and, in 2001, an estimated 1.7 million tourists visited Chile. Part of the attraction is that Chile is deemed to be a safe country, where transport is comfortable and runs on time, hotels are plentiful and cater for every kind of traveller, people are hospitable and the police helpful and reliable. But most of all, people visit Chile to see the remote and spectacular landscapes, with the extraordinary changes in scenery that take place from north to south of the country.

TRANSPORT

Chile's economic success is largely dependent on excellent transport and communications. Tourists can take the paved highway that runs unbroken for 3,078km from Arica to Puerto Montt. From there, the unpaved *Carretera Austral*, or Southern Highway, stretches over 1,000km to the tiny settlement of Villa O'Higgins in the far south. Numerous fjords south of Villa O'Higgins prevent a single non-stop route onwards to the Strait of Magellan.

Santiago is the hub of all transport in Chile. Long-distance coach services connect the capital with all the main towns in the north

Trekkers walking beside Lago Grey in the Towers of Paine National Park.

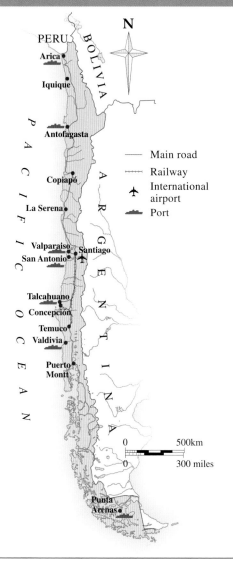

In June 2001 the Chilean government approved the construction of Line 4 of the Santiago Metro.

and south. Most towns and tourist centres are also well served by three domestic airlines, while other smaller carriers operate specialised routes. The main railway line runs south from Santiago to Temuco and Talcahuano, but there are few passenger rail services. Passengers on Santiago's metro make over 800,000 journeys per day on three lines. The metro is modern, clean, efficient and safe. Fares are the same for any length of journey but the rate is higher during rush hour (between 7.15 am and 9 am and 6 pm and 7.30 pm).

CASE STUDY
EASTER ISLAND

Often known as the world's most isolated island, Easter Island (see page 16) is 3,600km from the Chile mainland and 2,000km from Pitcairn, the nearest inhabited island. It derives its name from the date of its discovery, on Easter Sunday, 1722. In 1965 an airstrip was built, the isolation was broken, and now it is a top tourist destination. Hanga Roa, the main settlement, provides services such as hotels, car hire, trekking, diving, handicrafts, bars, restaurants and the Internet. There is a tsunami warning system, as the island has been struck several times. The 1960 earthquake that devastated parts of southern Chile caused a tsunami that raced across the Pacific at 800km/h and tore apart the island's sacred site of mysterious carved stone heads, or *moai*. The *moai* have since been re-erected.

The *Carretera Austral*, Ruta 7, runs south from Puerto Montt for 1,000 kilometres.

A vineyard thrives in the Central Valley, and pine plantations cover the slopes of the Cordillera de la Costa.

In the 1960s, land reform led to the break up of many large farms and estates and an increase in the number of small farmers. Although just 3 per cent of the country is given over to agriculture, there have been huge developments in farming since the 1970s. In every sector – wine, fruit, vegetables, fishing, forestry and livestock – production and exports have increased. Most farming takes places in the Central Valley, though large flocks of sheep are raised in the far south. Agriculture employs about 13.6 per cent of the work force and contributes about 6.4 per cent to GDP.

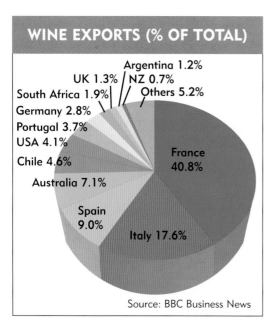

WINE EXPORTS (% OF TOTAL)

Argentina 1.2%
UK 1.3% / NZ 0.7%
South Africa 1.9% / Others 5.2%
Germany 2.8%
Portugal 3.7%
USA 4.1%
Chile 4.6%
Australia 7.1%
Spain 9.0%
France 40.8%
Italy 17.6%

Source: BBC Business News

THE HISTORY OF WINE

Spanish priests first introduced vines into Chile in the sixteenth century because they needed wine for religious celebrations. Vines were planted in the Central Valley around Santiago and grew well. In the 1850s, the Spanish vines were replaced by French varieties and winemaking became a serious industry. In the 1870s, the first Chilean wines were exported and, within 50 years, vineyards covered more than 100,000 hectares of land. During the twentieth century, the industry faced unusual difficulties. An alcohol law virtually banned the development of wineries or vineyards, and imports of winemaking machinery were impossible during World War II. The ban was repealed in 1974 and the industry modernised. At the same time traditional family owners

The natural barriers of the Andes, the Atacama Desert and the Pacific Ocean have given Chilean agriculture an enviable record. Passengers arriving at any frontier by air, sea or road have all their luggage checked for fruit, vegetables and dairy products. The reason for such caution is that the natural barriers have kept out two major pests: the Mediterranean fruit fly (medfly), that causes widespread damage to fruiting plants, and the insect *Dactulosphaira vitifolia*, that causes phylloxera. The latter damages the leaves and roots of vines. In the 1860s, phylloxera devastated the European wine industry, then quickly spread to vineyards worldwide. Today, Chile boasts the world's only pre-phylloxera vines and is the only country that has not been affected by the pest.

The fruit fly project is a success story in its own right. While the Central Valley was fly free, some flies bred in the far north in the Arica and Azapa valleys. These were eradicated by a 30-year programme of releasing thousands of specially bred, sterile flies into the zone. The option of using insecticidal spray was rejected in favour of the sterile breeding plan, which was less harmful to crops. Eventually the flies simply died out and, in 1995, the Arica and Azapa valleys were declared medfly free.

sold off many of their vineyards to large, often international, corporations.

THE PRODUCTION OF WINE

Most of Chile's vineyards are in the Central Valley, in the regions of the Maipo, Rapel, Curicó and Maule, where soil, sunlight, temperature and moisture conditions are perfect for growing vines. Historically, Chile has grown mostly the Cabernet Sauvignon grape, but recent successes with Merlot, Carmenere and Syrah grapes have made available a wider range of wines. Muscatel grapes are grown in the northern region, but principally for the national *pisco* drink.

The increase in the export of Chilean wine has been astonishing. In 1980, only 0.3 per cent of wine imported into the USA was from Chile. In 1999, this figure had reached 13 per cent and, by 2000, only Italy and France were exporting more wine to the USA than Chile. Between 1992 and 2002, wine exports shot up from $30m to over $600m per year. Chile is now the world's fifth-largest wine exporter.

Female workers sit alongside a conveyor belt checking bottles of wine.

FRUIT AND LIVESTOCK

Chile claims to be the world's largest exporter of table grapes. In the USA, 25 per cent of the grapes eaten are from Chile. But Chile's agricultural industry is also made up of a host of other fruit and vegetables, over 50 per cent of which are exported to the USA and Europe. Fruits include apples, avocados, peaches, nectarines, kiwi, plums, pears, blueberries and cherries, and the main vegetables are garlic, asparagus and onions.

As Chile is in the southern hemisphere, the fruits grown there are ready for export in northern hemisphere's winter season. In 2002, there were about 7,000 fresh fruit producers in Chile harvesting around 186,966 hectares of land. They produced 1.6 million tonnes of fresh fruits, or US$1.4 billion in exports, and sold to more than 70 countries around the world. With its long coastline and modern seaport and air facilities, Chile is in a good

A Chilean cowboy or *huaso* herds cattle and horses into stockyards in Temuco.

position to ensure that fruit arrives in foreign markets fresh and in good condition. Producers aim to get their fruit to a port within 24 hours of being picked. From there it is either shipped by sea on a 10 to 12 day trip, or sent overnight by air. Wheat, sugar beet, potatoes and maize are grown mainly for the domestic market.

SHEEP AND CATTLE

Chile exports poultry, pork and small amounts of lamb and beef. Exports of beef are set to rise as a result of free trade agreements with the USA and the European Union. To its advantage, Chile has remained free of foot-and-mouth disease. In 2002, Chile had 4.1 million head of cattle, 4.1 million sheep, 3.7 million pigs and 900,000 goats. The cattle stock is made up of European breeds: Holstein are the main dairy cattle, and beef cattle include Herefords, Aberdeen Angus, Shorthorn and many crossbreeds. The main sheep breeds are Corriedale and Merino.

About half the country's sheep stock is reared on *estancias* in the far south in Magallanes and Tierra del Fuego. These sheep account for about 60 per cent of Chile's wool production. The region also holds about 3 per cent of the national beef herd. Some farms are very large, with many thousand hectares extending across the grasslands. Some beef cattle and most dairy cattle are bred in the central region and in the northern part of southern Chile, while goats are found mainly in the north.

ANDEAN ANIMALS

For centuries, the Aymara and Quechua peoples have kept domesticated llamas as pack animals and alpacas for their wool. Two of the animals' relatives, the vicuña and guanaco have not been domesticated. In Inca times, the vicuña were herded into corrals and shorn once a year, and their very fine fur was kept for the sole use of the Inca emperor and his nobles. Today most of the vicuña and the larger herds of alpaca are found in Aymara regions high in the Andes. There are other herds of alpaca in Patagonia. Chilean law forbids vicuña hunting but they can be shorn, and some wool is exported to Argentina. The alpaca are largely sold as live animals to breeders worldwide, including the USA,

Alpaca in the high Andean *puna* of the Lauca National Park.

Australia and the UK. There is also a good domestic tourist market for sweaters, ponchos, gloves and other garments made in alpaca wool. Members of the Aymara communities and people from villages and towns in the north make many of the hand-knitted garments.

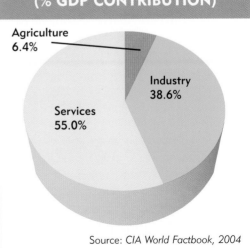

ECONOMIC STRUCTURE, 2004 (% GDP CONTRIBUTION)

Agriculture 6.4%

Industry 38.6%

Services 55.0%

Source: *CIA World Factbook, 2004*

FISHING

Chile's coastline is 6,435km long and the offshore waters are rich in fish, including many varieties of shellfish, mackerel, anchovy and herring. In the warmer waters around the Juan Fernández islands, lobster is the main catch.

The fishing industry took off in the 1970s and, by the early 1980s, Chile was the world's leading exporter of fishmeal. The fish catch increased dramatically from 1.2 million tonnes in 1970 to 6 million tonnes in 1991, when fishing exports exceeded US$1 billion for the first time. In the 1990s, the industry grew more than 10 per cent each year, and fishmeal continued to be the most important product. However, such intensive fishing has inevitably begun to threaten some species, such as the Patagonian toothfish, and the government has introduced measures to reduce overfishing and conserve stocks. In the 1990s there was considerable investment mainly by Chilean companies in fish farming. By 2001, Chile was the second-largest salmon producer in the world, with a production in that year of almost 254,000 tonnes. In 2002, the USA imported $400 million worth of farmed salmon from Chile, a 100 per cent increase from 1997.

ABOVE: Fishermen return to the port of Valparaiso and unload their early morning catch.

BELOW: Many varieties of fish, including shellfish, are sold in the daily fish market in Valdivia.

There are two known species of toothfish, the Patagonian *(Dissostichus eleginoides)* and the Antarctic *(D. mawsoni)*. The Patagonian toothfish is also known as Chilean sea bass, mero and Chilean grouper or black hake. It is a great delicacy, and fetches up to US$1,000 per fish. The USA and Japan are the main importers and Chile the main supplier. The fish grows slowly, reaching a length of more than 2m. A mature adult weighs more than 250 pounds. It can live for up to 50 years and does not breed until it is at least ten years old. It feeds largely on squid and prawns and itself forms a large part of the fish diet for sperm whales and elephant seals. It lives in waters between 300m and 3,500m deep, in the sub-Antarctic and southern parts of the Atlantic and Indian Oceans. Although the species is protected by law, many fish are caught illegally and there is a fear that the Patagonian toothfish could be extinct by 2007.

FORESTRY

Approximately a quarter of Chile is covered by forest. The most extensive areas of natural forest are the temperate southern beech *(Nothofagus* spp.*)* found in southern Chile, parts of neighbouring Argentina and Tierra del Fuego. Planted forests cover more than two million hectares. Ninety per cent of timber exports come from plantations that have replaced other crops on old agricultural land, but 10 per cent of the planted forests replace indigenous trees. From 1975, private companies were heavily subsidised by the state and were offered tax incentives to plant and exploit the forests. The majority of the plantations are pine *(Pinus radiata)* and eucalyptus. In 2002, about 38 million cubic metres of wood was cut. Instead of exporting raw logs, Chile uses mostly softwoods for the manufacture of forest products. It is the world's third-largest exporter of woodchips and also exports items such as milled boards, pulp, paper, furniture and hardboard.

A forestry worker cuts trees into lengths for transport to the woodchip mills.

New apartment blocks, homes for working and middle class people, built on a desert hill on the outskirts of Antofagasta.

Until the 1970s, Chile was renowned for its democratic and stable government. However, in 1973 General Pinochet seized power from an elected Marxist government led by President Salvador Allende. The Allende and Pinochet governments introduced reforms and counter-reforms that had a profound effect on Chilean society, which since colonial days had comprised a minority of very rich families and a majority of poor people.

RICH AND POOR

The level of poverty in Chile is still high, and there is a clear division between rich and poor. Since the end of military rule in 1989 and the return to democracy, social welfare has been high on the government agenda. Between 1989 and 2000, the number of Chileans living below the poverty line fell from about 39 per cent to 21 per cent. However, the distribution of income remains very unequal. In 2000, the wealthiest 10 per cent of the population received 40.3 per cent of national income, while the poorest 10 per cent received just 1.7 per cent.

HEALTH

Substantial investments in health programmes and in water and sanitation have helped reduce infant mortality rates and increase life expectancy. In urban areas, almost 100 per cent of the population now has access to water and proper sanitation. In rural areas, the figure is slightly reduced. People are living longer and fewer children are dying before they reach five years of age. In 1960, the mortality rate for under-fives was 155 deaths in every 1,000 births, in 2000 it was just 12, and by 2003 it had fallen to 9. This reduction is partly the result of widespread vaccination programmes against mumps, measles and whooping cough. Major diseases such as malaria and polio have been largely wiped out, though there was an outbreak of cholera in San Pedro de Atacama in 1998, and HIV/AIDS is increasing, especially among men.

Waiters serve at tables in a busy upmarket fish restaurant in Santiago's Central Market.

LIFE EXPECTANCY AT BIRTH

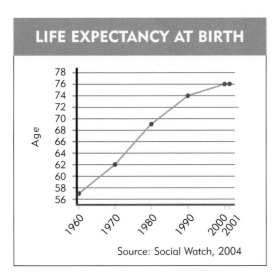

Source: Social Watch, 2004

A housing estate in the Central Valley, funded by the government for homeless 'people in need'.

The indigenous communities fare less well than other members of the population. They have a shorter life expectancy and many reject modern medicine in favour of traditional herbal medicines.

HOUSING

Wealthy Chileans have always lived in Santiago, and they have often also owned large ranches or *estancias* in the countryside. From the 1930s, as European, Jewish and Arab immigrants began to settle in the centre of the city, wealthy families moved out towards the Andean foothills. These suburbs now have shopping malls, leisure facilities and hospitals within easy reach. The large houses and spacious apartment blocks, with well tended gardens, contrast starkly with the poorest communities in Santiago, where houses are made from a variety of materials, including pine boards and cardboard. The majority of working- and middle-class families in Chilean towns and cities live in concrete or brick-built housing developments known as *poblaciones*. Houses in rural areas are generally quite basic, and in some places made of mud brick. *Palafitos* are wooden houses built on stilts to avoid flooding and they are unique to the island of Chiloé.

CASE STUDY
ARPILLERAS FOR THE DISAPPEARED

When the military were in power in Chile, making *arpilleras*, or pieces of brightly embroidered cloth carrying a strong political message, became part of a way of life for many poor women. Tens of thousands of men disappeared or were killed during the Pinochet regime, and the women – their mothers, sisters and wives – created *arpilleras* to tell the outside world what was happening. They depicted scenes with doll-like figures, perhaps showing a military raid, or torture, or they would write messages demanding bread and justice. The cloths were sold in many parts of the world until sales dwindled and the workshops shut down in the early 1990s.

UNDER-FIVE MORTALITY RATE

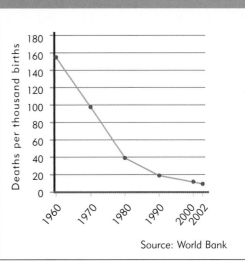

Source: World Bank

Aymara students in school. The Aymara are Chile's second-largest indigenous group.

EDUCATION

In Chile, schools, universities and other educational institutions are run by the state, the church, or funded privately. All children between the ages of six and fourteen are expected to attend primary school, and a law passed in 2003 made secondary schooling compulsory until the age of eighteen. The 2002 census reflected government efforts to improve education, showing that 99 per cent of children attended primary school. In 2002, the average length of schooling had increased from 7.5 years (in 1992) to 8.5 years.

Secondary schooling lasts for four years, and students are given the option of following either academic or technical courses. Students wishing to go on to university need to take an academic course

in either a science or an arts subject. Students following technical courses spend two years specialising in a particular subject, for example, industry, commerce or agriculture. Universities, professional institutes and technical training centres provide higher education, and the take up here almost doubled between 1992 and 2002, from 9 to 16.4 per cent. The literacy level in Chile is high, at over 95 per cent. The lowest literacy levels are found among the indigenous communities in rural areas, where schools and educational facilities are less accessible.

In colonial times, parish priests set out on the first Sunday after Easter to take the Holy Sacraments to the sick and elderly. They were accompanied by *huasos*, or cowboys, who protected them, and the silver chalices they carried, from bandits. The custom has continued with the Fiesta of Cuasimodo, which takes place in many parts of the Central Valley. As well as cowboys, priests are accompanied today by children and adults, the *cuasimodistas*, on bicycles, and by horses decorated with flowers and ribbons. The priests ride in carriages decorated with lilies, and the *cuasimodistas* wear white capes with yellow decoration, and cover their heads with white handkerchiefs.

A traditionally dressed *huaso* takes part in a riding contest during the Fiesta of Cuasimodo.

RELIGION

In the sixteenth century, Spanish priests and missionaries introduced Roman Catholicism to Chile and it has been the main religion ever since. Today, about 70 per cent of the population over the age of fourteen regard themselves as Catholics, but only 25 per cent of them attend church regularly. The number is declining as Protestants and Evangelicals, now about 15 per cent of the population, increase. Less than 5 per cent of the population practise other religions, and they include Jews, Muslims and sects such as Mormons, who instead of the Bible follow the *Book of Mormon*. A growing number of Chileans follow no religion.

Catholicism is still predominantly taught in school, and a celebration of Mass frequently marks public events. National holidays in Chile reflect the Christian calendar, celebrating Christmas, Easter, Corpus Christi in June, the Assumption in August, and All Saints' Day in November. Celebrations also take place on specific saints' days and the Fiesta of Cuasimodo takes place in many parts of central Chile.

In a traditional Roman Catholic ceremony, a priest blesses a newly married couple.

FAMILY LIFE

Family ties in Chile are strong. When people marry they are expected to set up their own households, but they still remain close to their families. Children are brought up to know their cousins, aunts and uncles, and families spend time together. Generations also remain very close, with grandparents often helping with young children while parents go out to work. At the same time, children are expected to respect and help their elderly relatives. Friends are often included in the extended family, and godparents take their responsibilities seriously. Everyone gets together to celebrate family occasions, such as baptisms and weddings.

THE ROLE OF WOMEN

Chilean women only gained the right to vote in 1949. For many years, a woman's role in the

The family unit is very important in Chile. Only 8.1 per cent of Chileans live alone.

family was that of traditional wife and mother. Divorce was illegal until 2003, but the law has been changed and now divorce can follow after one year's separation, if both parties agree. Much else has changed too, and today women represent about a third of the workforce. This is largely the result of more education for women, particularly in the area of higher education and training for professional jobs. Many women work as teachers, nurses, social workers, and in commerce, and increasing numbers are qualifying as doctors and lawyers. About half the country's judges are women. Employing domestic servants in the home

There are now many female professionals in Chile's workforce.

FEMALE LABOUR FORCE

% of total labour force

Year	%
1965	23
1975	24
1985	28
1995	32
2000	34
2001	34

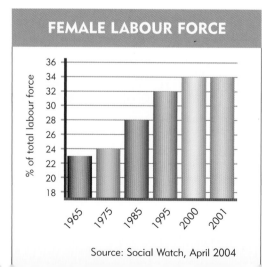

Source: Social Watch, April 2004

CASE STUDY
CURANTO

Women preparing a curanto meal with meat, shellfish and vegetables cooked in panque leaves.

Curanto is a dish traditional to the indigenous people from Chiloé and the south. Red hot stones are placed in a hole in the ground about 1.5m deep. The stones are covered with large leaves, and the ingredients placed on the leaves. They include a mix of shellfish, beef, chicken, smoked pork and chorizo, peas, beans, potatoes, pumpkin, and some specially prepared potato breads. The food is covered by another layer of leaves, and sacks of potatoes and wet flour sacks are laid on top. The food is left to cook for about an hour, or until steam rises from the ground. Then it is opened up and everyone shares the meal.

makes it easier for women to work, and there are a good number of pre-school and day-care facilities for babies and toddlers. There has also been a change of attitude among men, many of whom, polls indicate, now support the idea of women going out to work.

FOOD

With such a long coastline, it is not surprising that Chileans enjoy a wide variety of fish, ranging from shellfish to *congrio* (conger eel), which is the national dish. *Caldillo de congrio* is a type of soup served with a piece of conger, onions and potato. For people living along the coast, fish is part of the daily diet. For centuries, indigenous people have grown and eaten corn and it is still the basis of many dishes, such as *humitas*, mashed corn wrapped in vine or cabbage leaves and steamed, or *pastel de choclo*, which is rather like a cottage pie with mashed corn instead of potato. Meat is also plentiful and is most popular barbecued over hot embers. Like their Argentine neighbours, Chileans eat all cuts of meat, including intestines and brains. Soup is the favourite dish during the cold winter months. A soup or *cazuela* may be based on meat, fish or chicken with added ingredients of potato, pumpkin, corn and peppers. Fruit and vegetables are plentiful in Chile, and snacks include *empanadas*, a pastry filled with meat, onions, peppers, raisins and olives.

EARNING A LIVING

After many years of high unemployment, the economic improvements of the late 1980s produced a remarkable change. By the middle of the 1990s, Chile had its lowest ever rate of unemployment, at less than 5 per cent. However, in 1999 Chile entered a period of recession, mainly caused by a fall in the world price for copper. Many people lost their jobs. Afterwards, unemployment remained consistently high: in 2003 it was 8.5 per cent, even though the economy had largely recovered. The government has introduced measures to try to increase the income of skilled and semi-skilled workers, but the GDP per capita is still low. For 2003, it was an estimated US$10,274.

The thousands of unqualified and unskilled workers who arrive in the towns from rural areas often struggle to earn a living. Some find work as domestic servants, or as labourers in construction or in the manufacturing industries,

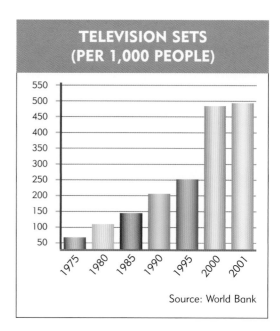

TELEVISION SETS (PER 1,000 PEOPLE)

Source: World Bank

About 100,000 people are employed in Chile's fishing and fish-farming industries. Most own or work on the boats supplying the local markets.

but a great many finish up selling odds and ends on the streets. They are counted as employed because they have an income. The government has tried to control the street trade (in Santiago it is limited to certain areas), but with only partial success.

TIME OFF

Santiago is within easy reach of the mountains and the sea. During the winter, people head for the mountains to ski on the slopes near the Argentine border, and in the summer crowds fill the beaches in Viña del Mar and other resorts. There are opportunities for most kinds of watersports, although many of these are too expensive for poorer people. In the north, Arica and Antofagasta have good beaches, while in the south the Lake District is ideal for camping, hiking, trekking and walking.

Like most Latin Americans, Chileans are passionate about football, which was introduced by British immigrants in the early 1800s. The best teams are in Santiago, and there are regular league matches and competitions. There are facilities for most popular sports, such as tennis, which received a great boost when the men's singles and doubles team won Chile's first ever Olympic gold medals in 2004.

Chile's most important national holiday is Independence Day on 18 September, followed by Army Day on 19 September. There are parades, festivities, music, food, drink and demonstrations of the national dance, the *cueca*. The *huasos*, or cowboys, wear their finest gear and the ladies dress in full skirts and shawls. They perform the dance, a form of courtship ritual, with much waving of handkerchiefs and jangling of spurs. In the background, guitarists strum romantic melodies. Independence Day also marks the beginning of the rodeo season that continues until March.

Children dance the *cueca* at the Independence Day celebrations in Chillán.

CASE STUDY
RODEOS

Rodeos are perhaps the most popular pastime in Chile. They originate from the days when *huasos* rounded up cattle for branding or slaughter. The *huasos* of the rodeo are always finely attired in richly woven ponchos, broad-brimmed hats, silk sashes, high-heeled leather boots, carved wooden stirrups and large silver spurs. They ride magnificent horses. The rodeo begins with a judges' inspection of the horses and riders, who then compete in a display of horsemanship and demonstrate teamwork in controlling young cattle. Rodeo competitions take place throughout the season and culminate in the national championships in Rancagua. For spectators, rodeos are a great day out. There is much to eat and drink, and the day finishes with music and dancing.

Rodeos take place almost every week in southern Chile during the season from September to March.

Early morning desert fog, the *camanchaca*, hangs over the Atacama Desert near Chanaral.

Chile has many unique habitats for plants and wildlife, but the rapid advance of the economy has, in places, endangered the environment. Problems include pollution caused by the by-products of mining, intensive agriculture, tourism or personal motor transport. Whatever the causes, many parts of the country are now threatened.

LIFE IN THE DESERT

In the Atacama Desert plants and animals have adapted to the climate, and conserve every drop of moisture. Some areas are so dry that nothing seems to be living, yet beneath the surface are specialised insects, small reptiles and mammals that emerge in the cool of the night. Cacti survive below ground, as do plant seeds which remain dormant, waiting for a rainstorm. In less barren areas, tall cacti grow in canyons; and plant communities called *lomas* develop in zones dampened by the *camanchaca* fog. *Lomas* consist of many ground-hugging species and a few bushes.

Higher in the mountains, the plants are highly specialised. One plant, the *llareta*, is a relative of parsley, and is so tough, compact and resinous that people use it, illegally, for fuel. There are few mammals in these places. Small groups of vicuñas inhabit the high, arid *puna* grasslands, and

On the slopes of Volcán Parinacota, in the Lauca National Park, vicuña graze on the high *puna* bogs.

guanaco are found both in high altitudes and in the lower *lomas* zones. The largest bird in Chile is the rhea, which resembles a small ostrich. Among the high Andean volcanoes, a few isolated salty lakes attract waterbirds and there are patches of specialised, hardy vegetation. Some of these areas have been designated sites of special scientific importance. The Laguna del Negro Francisco and Laguna Santa Rosa, two small lakes more than 3,715m above sea level, are home to three species of flamingo and the rare horned coot, which builds nests on mounds of stones that it gathers and piles on the lake bed.

THE RICH SEA

The cool Humboldt current, which moves north through the Pacific Ocean along the coast, carries many nutrients and is one of the richest currents in the world. These plentiful nutrients support the growth of enormous quantities of plankton (tiny plant and animal organisms that inhabit the surface layer of the ocean). The plankton, in turn, provides food for other marine life and gives the Chilean coastal water its abundance of fish and crustaceans. Quotas for fishing exist, but in reality these are exceeded. Exceeding the quotas may upset the balance, particularly in years when El Niño (see page 17) also causes a reduction in the water's nutrients. The dumping of large quantities of mineral waste

The world's rarest flamingo, the James flamingo, is found on salt lakes in Chile and Bolivia.

from mines also affects the coastal water. Almost everywhere, there is some kind of contamination from the effects of rapid economic growth.

CASE STUDY
DESERTIFICATION

Goats are the principal cause of the desertification of land in the Coquimbo region, about 400km north of Santiago. Here, the economy of about 100,000 people in 115 communities depends on the countryside. The people grow wheat and keep goats for milk and meat. Unfortunately goats will eat almost anything; they take green and dry plants, and quickly clear small shrubs until the ground is bare. Their tiny hooves scuff the soil and then compact it, so the surface becomes hard and useless. The people of the Coquimbo region are well aware of the problem because their wheat yields have fallen. Agricultural experts have offered advice and financial help for better management of the animals. These include planting bushes for food and finding ways of controlling the goats.

UNIQUE ANIMALS AND PLANTS

Many of the 450 plant species found in the rainforest are native to Chile. The trees vary according to the region, with the Chile pines appearing only in the northern Andean part of the rainforest zone. Elsewhere the forest is composed of southern beeches, laurels, myrtles and conifers, including the *alerce*. Among the oldest trees in the world, *alerces* can reach 30 to 40m. Their wood is highly valued, and a large tree can fetch thousands of dollars. In the past settlers cut down the trees at random, but now *alerces* have national monument status and felling them is illegal.

The high rainfall promotes an exuberant growth in the closed canopy forest, which includes many lianas, ferns, climbing shrubs and bromeliads. Chile's national flower, the *copihue*, is also found in the rainforest. A relative of the lily, it is a protected species. Darwin's fungus, named after the famous scientist and explorer, is a globular orange mass found on the trees in the south, and was collected by indigenous peoples as food. Another namesake, the unusual Darwin's frog, has vocal sacs that are not only used for singing but also structured to hold the eggs laid by the female. The world's smallest deer,

COOL RAINFORESTS

The world's most southerly rainforests are in Chile. They are classified as cool-temperate rainforest because the annual rainfall is between 1,400 and 4,900mm and the January temperature is 16°C. About 9 to 10 per cent of the rain falls in the summer months. These forests occur in a remarkable ecological pocket stretching down the coast from a point close to Temuco to Cape Horn in the far south.

The Andean Condor is one of the world's largest birds, with a wingspan of up to 2.9m.

The Chilean pine, or monkey puzzle tree, occurs naturally only in Chile where it grows to a height of over 30m. It bears whorls of thin branches covered with dark-green ovate and sharply pointed leaves. First recorded in 1795, the monkey puzzle tree was introduced to Europe where it soon became a curiosity and found its way into private and public gardens. In the 1800s, an Englishman was supposed to have said that the tree would be a puzzle for a monkey to climb – hence its common name. In its native Chile it is known as the *araucaria* after its long connection with the Araucanian tribes, which include the surviving Mapuche and Pehuenche. The seeds of the *araucaria* are pine nuts, or *piñones*, and have been a part of the wild food of the Pehuenche for centuries. They are still collected and, for the surviving Pehuenche, both the tree and its seeds are sacred and an important element of their modest economy.

A monkey puzzle tree, with Volcán Lonquimay in the background.

the *pudu*, can also be found in the rainforest. Standing no taller than about 50cm at the shoulder, the *pudu* has a maximum weight of about 13 to 15 kilos. It favours bamboo thickets, and is mainly nocturnal.

ALIVE IN THE LAND OF FIRE

The western part of Chilean Tierra del Fuego is a wilderness of islands, narrow channels and mountains. Almost all of it is protected within two national parks, the Parque Nacional Alberto M. de Agostini and Parque Nacional Hernando de Magallanes. Cool, temperate rainforest covers the lower parts of the mountains and cold, boggy areas with trees in sheltered places fringe the western side. The shoreline is largely rock with numerous isolated bays and inlets, inaccessible except by sea. Colonies of Magellan penguins attract the tourists, but there are many other birds to be seen, ranging from flamingos to hummingbirds. The varied though sparse fauna also includes elephant seals, the Fuegian fox (sometimes known as the Andean wolf), a burrowing rodent called the *tucu tucu*, two species of bat and the rare marine otter.

THE PRESSURE OF PEOPLE

Although environmental concerns seem remote in the apparent wilderness of Chile, the rapid growth of the economy is causing pollution problems in the Central Valley and other areas. Chemicals are used as fertilisers and in pest-controlling sprays; forests have been cleared for farmland; the rivers have serious pollution problems; and the rubbish disposal crisis is growing. Pollution has also been increased by the rapid expansion of the fish farming industry, which uses chemicals to control fish diseases and pests such as sea lice.

POLLUTION FROM MINING

In mining, the processes of extraction and the digging out of huge amounts of minerals have resulted in several environmental problems. These include the emission into the atmosphere of particle waste, and metal pollution of water supplies. Arsenic occurs naturally in the Atacama. This means that many water supplies are affected, and sometimes the level rises for no apparent reason. The Chilean authorities have begun monitoring the water for the main cities, and samples from the Loa River are checked daily. When residents of Chiu Chiu near Calama complained of physical symptoms, such as pains and skin blotches, the amount of arsenic per litre of drinking water was found to be many times over the internationally recognised limit. The mining process also produces millions of tonnes of useless rock, which have to be dumped. The smelters create smoke that needs to be cleaned, and the concentration of powerful lights for night work has resulted in light pollution of what used to be one of the world's clearest night skies.

Emissions from the smelters in the Chuquicamata copper mine contribute significantly to pollution in the Atacama Desert.

ALL CHANGE IN THE FOREST

Timber ranks high in the investment plans of Chilean and foreign businessmen. But statistics for the industry say that the natural forest will have virtually disappeared in twenty years' time. Environmentalists also warn of the effects of inroads being made on the remote forests of Tierra del Fuego. Businessmen argue that the natural forests are being replaced with tens of thousands of pine and eucalyptus trees, which absorb carbon dioxide and prevent erosion. The trees also grow quickly and can be cropped frequently. However, it is not yet known what effect this change of habitat will have upon the wildlife that has inhabited the native, natural forests for a very long time.

As tree trunks are stacked ready for transport, the arguments about the hazards and benefits of intensive forestry farming rage on.

CASE STUDY
POLLUTION IN SANTIAGO

By Latin-American standards, Santiago is a small city but it is one of the most polluted on the continent. This is partly because of its location in a depression between the mountains, and because of emissions of polluting gases, such as sulphur dioxide and nitrogen dioxide, produced by industry and by the hundreds of thousands of vehicles that travel in the city daily. Trapped inside the hollow depression, the cool, smog-laden air covers the city like a blanket. The Metropolitan Environmental Health Service publishes a daily bulletin of air pollution levels. At times, the smog is so bad that it is necessary to restrict traffic from entering the city, and businesses close for the day. Santiago's pollution problems do not end here. The rush to economic growth has meant that sewage, industrial effluent and rubbish disposal has not kept pace with demand. The city's rivers are highly contaminated and the three major rubbish tips are full. At last, however, recycling programmes have started and some progress is being made.

A view of Santiago covered in smog, with the snow-capped Andes Mountains in the background.

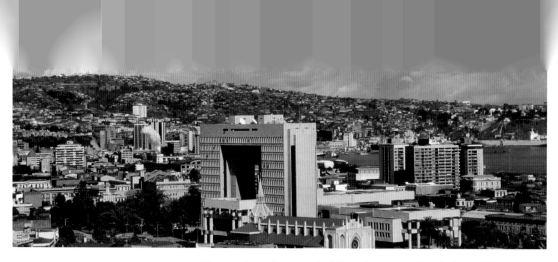

The modern Congress building dominates the skyline of Valparaiso.

C hile is a country with a vast range of resources. It is immensely rich in reserves of copper, and other minerals; its extensive coastal waters have plentiful stocks of fish; its forest plantations provide for the timber industry; and its agricultural sector continues to grow. The natural beauty and huge diversity of this extraordinarily shaped country also attract good numbers of tourists. But, to maintain progress, Chile needs to plan carefully and resolve its energy and environmental problems.

TELECOMMUNICATIONS

In the 1990s, Chile invested heavily in the telecommunications industry, which is now well advanced in comparison with other Latin American countries. In the second half of the decade, Chile invested US$1 billion dollars annually, 40 per cent of which went into the mobile phone market. By 2001, 3.8 million subscribed to mobile phones compared with 3.5 million with fixed telephone lines. New fibre-optic cable links have also improved Chile's communications with the rest of the world.

In 2000, the number of Internet users rose by almost 30 per cent, to 1.8 million. The Internet is the fastest-growing part of the

Internet cafes are found in most towns. They are inexpensive and widely used by students.

On 11 September 2003, the enormous hole in the ozone layer above the Antarctic measured 28 million square km. Newspapers, radio and television warned that seven minutes spent in the sunlight between the hours of 11 am and 3 pm could result in harmful levels of radiation. The ozone depletion danger is not of Chile's making but the result of worldwide use of chemicals known as CFCs. These chemicals are largely used in aerosols and refrigerators. When CFCs were discovered to be damaging, they were banned and replacements were found. Now only the oldest refrigerators use the banned CFCs and great care is taken to dispose of them safely.

The Chileans, who stand to be more affected than most by the hole in the ozone layer, have also taken measures to cease the use of methyl bromide, a pesticide used in fruit farming. Methyl bromide has been used around the world for the last 40 years to control microbes, insects and rodents, and Chileans have used it extensively. With the help of the United Nations Development Programme and others, a scheme has been set up to gradually phase out methyl bromide and replace it with other technologies. The aim is to eliminate the use of methyl bromide worldwide by 2015, and it is hoped that, with other similar actions, the ozone hole will heal by 2050.

ABOVE: Santiago's tallest building is the CTC building, headquarters of Telefonica, one of Chile's major telephone services.

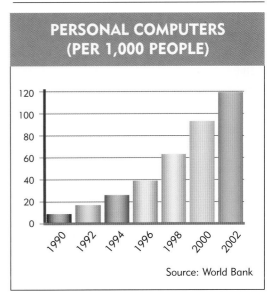

PERSONAL COMPUTERS (PER 1,000 PEOPLE)

Source: World Bank

TELECOMMUNICATIONS DATA, 2002 (PER 1,000 PEOPLE)

Mainline phones	230
Mobile phones	428
Internet users	238

Source: World Bank

country's communications sector. A study by the University of Chile identified most users as educated, upper class and aged between 15 and 34 years. Anxious that the digital revolution should not create further divisions in society, the state makes subsidies available to Internet centres in rural areas and to low-income urban communities. The state is also helping to promote a scheme in which businesses work together to establish community centres that use recycled computers equipped with Internet access. An example of how the Internet has helped the country's economy is the state-of-the-art electronic tracking and booking system used by the national airline, LAN, which speeds up the export of Chilean products.

The port of Arica in northern Chile handles most of the imports and exports to neighbouring Bolivia.

ENERGY AND ENVIRONMENT

While Chile's mineral resources seem safe and plentiful for many years to come, the country has to rely for its energy on the relatively small oil, gas and coal supplies in the south and on hydroelectric plants yet to be built. Chile already imports oil and gas, mainly from Argentina. The most immediately convenient solution would be to import gas from neighbouring Bolivia. But, despite the fact that Bolivia has sufficient gas for its needs for a thousand years, the Bolivians do not want to sell it to Chile. The hostility between the two countries can be traced back to the War of the Pacific in 1870, when Bolivia lost a section of the Atacama Desert and its only port on the

Pacific coast to Chile. Bolivia is now landlocked and, although it has permission to trade through the port of Arica, it refuses to sell gas to Chile until the problem is more permanently resolved. In the meantime, Chile could look to Venezuela, which has the second-largest gas reserves in South America.

NATIONAL PARKS

The Chilean government has established 31 national parks (NP), 48 national reserves (NR) and 15 natural monuments (NM) in an effort to protect Chile's biodiversity, a unique natural resource. Chile has also signed the RAMSAR convention, which agrees to protect wetlands, including some lakes, marshes and coastal lagoons.

Some national parks, such as the high Andean lagunas, are remote, but others are close to tourist centres in the Lake District. Corporación Nacional Forestal (CONAF), the government agency responsible, aims at protection, education, and providing an environment for recreation and facilities for eco-tourism. Santiago has four protected areas within easy reach. In the Cordillera de la Costa to the north-west, the NP of La Campana protects some of the last remaining Chilean palms. Nearest to the capital, the NR of Rio Clarillo protects the headwaters of one of the rivers flowing to the city. It also protects specialised mountain forests. Rio Los Cipreses NP is 100km to the south-east of Santiago, and the NM El Morado,

A geologist working in the Atacama Desert uses modern technology to search for mineral deposits.

NATIONAL PARKS AND OTHER PROTECTED AREAS

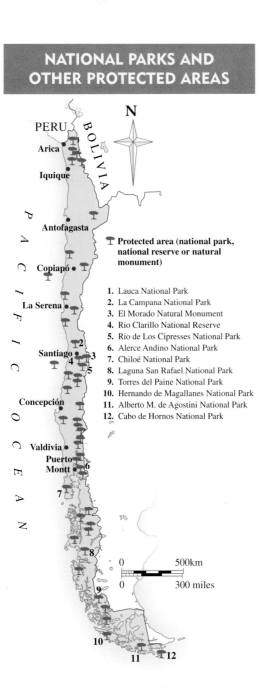

Protected area (national park, national reserve or natural monument)

1. Lauca National Park
2. La Campana National Park
3. El Morado Natural Monument
4. Rio Clarillo National Reserve
5. Rio de Los Cipresses National Park
6. Alerce Andino National Park
7. Chiloé National Park
8. Laguna San Rafael National Park
9. Torres del Paine National Park
10. Hernando de Magallanes National Park
11. Alberto M. de Agostini National Park
12. Cabo de Hornos National Park

0   500km

0   300 miles

The Salto del Indio (Indian Falls) is a 60m waterfall surrounded by temperate forest in the Lake District.

with a peak of 5,060m, is one-and-a-half hours' drive east of the city.

While CONAF has established several protected areas within the cool temperate forest zone, a massive private park has been created south of Puerto Montt. Known as the Pumalin Park, it is the world's largest privately owned conservation area, and the brainchild of a multimillionaire North American who has formed a Chilean Foundation to take care of the land. Some sections of Pumalin Park are now open to the public.

The richness of the Humboldt current has inspired the creation of an underwater park near Viña del Mar on the coast. Diving is supervised in three sections, from the very shallowest waters to one deep route. Visitors can see a variety of marine life, ranging from anemones and sponges to rays and many species of fish.

In the far south a spectacular park, a reserve and a national monument are set among the eroded Andes. At the Towers of Paine, hardy tourists can watch condors and guanaco. The NP Cabo de Hornos is the most southerly park, with its 406m-high central hill, low, dense vegetation, seabirds and mammals. These areas have been set apart for their ecosystems and, in the case of the most distant, Easter Island, to bring environment and history together. In the present century, with an ever-shrinking natural world beyond its frontiers, Chile is making great efforts to safeguard its heritage for future generations.

Alpaca A domesticated animal related to the llama. The alpaca is native to the Andes and much valued for its wool.

Archipelago A group of islands.

Biodiversity The variety of biological life within an area.

Colony The settlement of people from one country in another land, or a land or region governed by another country.

Conquistador Spanish word for an adventurer or explorer who sets out to conquer another nation.

Consumer A person who buys or acquires items for domestic use, such as food, clothing, cars and household goods.

Continental plates Large areas of the Earth's crust, floating on top of a more fluid (liquid) layer.

Dictator A person, usually the head or ruler of a country, who governs completely and often ruthlessly.

Drought Lack of rain over a long period of time.

Eco-tourism Tourism that is sensitive to its impact on environments and local population.

Environment Surroundings, especially the natural world.

Estancia A large farm.

Fjord A long, deep, narrow arm of the sea, running up between high banks or cliffs, which are often snow-covered.

Free trade The movement of goods freely between countries, without the restriction of import taxes.

GDP (Gross Domestic Product) The monetary value of goods and services produced by a country in a single year.

Geothermal power Energy derived from the heat contained in rocks deep within the Earth's crust, or from hot springs or volcanoes.

Geyser A hot spring that throws up water or steam from under the ground in active or recently active volcanic regions.

GNI (Gross National Income) The monetary value of goods and services produced by a country plus any earnings from overseas in a single year. It used to be called Gross National Product (GNP).

Guanaco A wild relative of the llama and the alpaca, and native to the Andean countries of South America.

Habitat The natural home of a living plant or animal.

Headwaters The streams from the sources of a river.

HEP (hydroelectric power) Electricity generated by using the power of water.

Immigrant A person who moves to a new country and settles there.

Inca People who ruled present day Peru, and parts of Bolivia, Argentina, Chile and Ecuador before the arrival of the Spaniards early in the sixteenth century.

Indigenous Born or produced naturally in a land or region; person who is native to a land or region.

Life expectancy The expected number of years that a person will live.

Marxist A follower of the theories of the German Socialist Karl Marx (1818–1883).

Mestizos People of mixed Native American and Spanish or Portuguese ancestries.

Metropolitan Of or relating to a large city.

Plateau A high, flat area of land.

Pollution The poisoning of land, water or air by human activity such as industry, transportation, or agriculture.

Production The part of a country's economy where products are manufactured, mined or cultivated.

Prospector A person who explores a region for gold, diamonds or something similar.

Puna A bleak, usually very high, upland in the Andes Mountains.

Rainforest Dense forest with high rainfall.

Recession A temporary decline or setback in economic activity.

Refinery An industrial site where substances such as oil or sugar are refined.

Reservation A tract of land set aside by a government for some special purpose, or for certain persons such as a native tribe.

Seismometer An instrument for measuring the intensity, direction, and duration of earthquakes.

Services Economic activities that are paid for although nothing is produced, such as tourism and banking.

Smog A combination of the words 'smoke' and 'fog', describing a mixture of pollutants in the air.

Synchronise To occur at the same time.

Temperate A mild climate type without great extremes of heat and cold.

Tsunami A huge sea wave occasionally experienced along coasts, caused by an earthquake or volcanic activity.

Aymara llama herders drive their animals through a mountain pass in the Andes between Bolivia and Chile.

FURTHER INFORMATION

BOOKS TO READ:

In Focus: Chile by Nick Caistor (Latin American Bureau/ Interlink Books NY, 1998) An overview of the people, politics, economy, society and culture of Chile.

Rough Guide to Chile by Melissa Graham (Rough Guides Ltd, 2nd edition 2003) A budget travel guide for travellers of all ages.

In Patagonia by Bruce Chatwin (Vintage/Penguin, 2003) A cult travel book about Patagonia, though it concentrates more on Argentina.

Between Extremes: A Journey Beyond Imagination by Brian Keenan and John McCarthy (Black Swan/Corgi/ Transworld Pub Inc., 2000) An account of a journey from Arica to Tierra del Fuego made five years after Keenan and McCarthy were released from captivity in Beirut.

Voyage of the Beagle by Charles Darwin (Penguin/Wordsworth Editions Ltd, 1997) An abridged version of Darwin's journey around the world in 1831, that contains interesting descriptions of Chile from Tierra del Fuego to Iquique.

The House of Spirits by Isabel Allende (Black Swan/ Bantam Books, 1985) A fantastical, fiction story based in Chile before a military coup and murder of the president. (Isabel Allende is the niece of the murdered Chilean president, Salvador Allende.)

Saddled With Darwin by Toby Green (Phoenix, 2000) An excellent account of rural Chile.

WEBSITES:

GENERAL INFORMATION ON CHILE:
www.cia.gov/cia/publications/factbook/geos/ci.html
www.nationsonline.org/oneworld/chile.htm

WILDLIFE:
www.alpaca-uk.co.uk/aboutalpacas.htm

PEOPLE:
www.mapuche-nation.org

TOURISM:
www.lonelyplanet.com
www.visit-chile.org/portada/home.phtml

INDUSTRY:
www.codelcoeduca.cl
In Spanish, an animated educational site about the copper industry.

Numbers shown in **bold** refer to pages with maps, graphic illustrations or photographs

Wooden *palafito* houses, built on stilts to avoid flooding, are now only found on the island of Chiloé.

Boys playing football in the
late evening, with Puerto
Montt and Volcán Osorno in
the background.